The thread of Light

A. Sw. Bie

For the One in All

Caterpillar crawls

always busy
always hungry for more

A Radiant One watches silently
Caterpillar knows it not

Butterfly rests softly on the
petals of a flower

Its shimmering wings
catch the rays of sun

bursting into rare beauty

For a moment
all is still

Time is suspended in a hush

and even the sun
makes a halt in its path

A slight tremble of its wings
then butterfly lifts off

Only the gentle swaying of a flower left

Caterpillar crawls
having seen or heard nothing

Its occupation leaves no room for wonder

Oblivious of the revelation
it is heading for the next leaf

I have a habit of finding jewels. Not diamonds or sapphires and usually not the most precious metals either but the more common versions – small bits and pieces; a tiny crystal, half an earring, a pearl, a broken bracelet or part of a brooch – all of them creations of beauty lost in the hurry and events of life.

It is really not me who finds them but they who find me. I do not look for them. I am actually not looking for anything at all, just being on my way to wherever that happens to be, when out of the corner of my eye I will suddenly catch a *glimpse*.

Something calls me. It's like a vivid beam of Light focused in my direction and seeking my attention. It all happens in an instant. The flash is registered and gone at the same moment, and if I do not respond immediately, I will miss the opportunity and the incident will be forgotten, almost before I become conscious of it.

This shimmer of Light is not the glossy, superficial kind of glare that bounces off smooth or polished surfaces. It is a deliberate ray of Light, reaching straight to my core.

I have learnt to take notice of these glimpses and pick up the trodden-upon treasures. To me they are tiny messengers, reminders of the World of Light.

There is nothing complicated about Light. So clear and pure, unpretentious and serene, we may pass it by unnoticed.

And yet, the World of Light has been subject to great mystification. The simple testimonies of the Messengers have been twisted until hardly recognizable. Speculations have flourished, confusing and bewildering more than aiding our understanding. Basic truths have been lost in a maelstrom of non-essentials.

Light is simple.

Mostly the intellectual mind despises all that is not intricate and convoluted, mistaking simplicity for superficiality, or even banality.

Only to the hasty glance do they look the same.

The World of Light has never been hidden and is not to be found in some distant place. It is an age-old habit of perceiving divisions that prevents us from sensing its Presence.

Unlike our fragmented sight, the World of Light is seamless and undividable. It is always concerned with the Whole and knows no separate agenda.

Somewhere along the ancient path of history, a misunderstanding occurred. It was due to an error of perception and inevitable, as it was much too dark to see clearly.

In the gloom of the past we fell under a magic spell.

Mesmerized by moving shadows on the cave walls, we started to perceive Life in fragments, as unrelated, isolated bits.

Confused, the mind invented a concept of a separate, broken self, not realizing it was only seeing a mirage.

Fully immersed in this state of illusion, where everything appears as sharply cut apart, we no longer recognized our kin and started viewing each other as strangers and enemies.

And so we forgot. Not even remembering that it was something we had forgotten. Something crucially important.

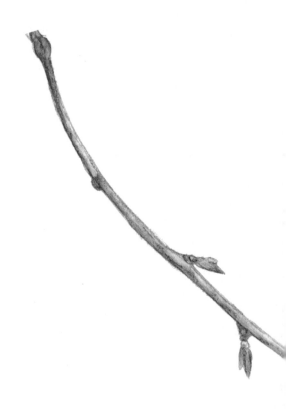

A mirror lost

broken

scattered throughout
in shimmering dust

faded into dull
forgotten memories

veiled behind

a multitude of
eyes

A billion scars

lives fallen by the wayside

and hardly a tear
to speak for this misery

I am The Unspoken

the Stillness behind
a roar of voices

I am The Yet Unborn

looking for My reflection
in a world of fragments

Still My lines are too fine for your senses
My voice too subtle for your mind

how easy to brush past in a hurry
how easy for you to ignore

so unseen
so unheard of

Yet, I Am

Little does the caterpillar know

Crawling among leaves
unaware of even the smallest flower

nodding

Without Light, no development would be possible. We would have remained embedded in darkness, unable to unfold our latent possibilities. There would have been no new insights, no enlightened thoughts and no illumined discoveries.

Unable to advance, to expand our range of vision and become aware of previously unrecognized vistas of reality, we would have been relegated to the dark and dimly lit areas, prisoners of fear, ignorance, superstition and blind beliefs.

Light reveals. By illuminating the different areas of life with ever-brightening Light, more of reality becomes visible to us.

And as matters are infused with higher potencies of Light, the myriads of forms through which Life expresses itself are gradually lifted and developed into greater awareness, diversity and beauty.

This urge to evolve, to refine and expand beyond the present limitations, is running steadfast and patiently and sure through the eons. It is the very nature of Life itself, seeking always a greater and more complete expression of its true potential.

Messengers of Light always seek to impart a larger view and a greater sense of the real and the true. In this way the path towards increasing Light is illumined and we become able to perceive the next step.

It is always a challenge to see in brighter Light, as the established norms will be disturbed. The stronger the Light, the more difficult it is to take, and often we resist and repel its influence.

Light brings the hidden out of the dark and gives clarity and sanity of mind. It does not shroud in mystery but makes the evident clear.

The mind is cunning.

Its old propensity for make-believe can easily make black appear like white or true like false, according to expediency. The admiration for the complex can leave it totally blind to the glaringly obvious, and the readily achievable may seem like unsolvable knots.

Having mistaken the true Self for a transient speck of dust, it is conditioned to seeing everything in a distorted way.

But it's silly to be fooled by one's own mind, isn't it?

It is not easy for the mind to awaken from the ancient spell. It fears its own undoing.

But at long last, it will start to feel constricted within too narrow a vision. Suffering the absence of a real purpose, it yearns for *something else*.

Something not of its own making.

There comes a day
when caterpillar spins itself a nest

The restless creeping and crawling ceases

Weary of leaves
it turns its desire in a new direction

hidden within its cave

Sealed and cradled in the
midst of darkness

caterpillar dreams

A dream of
luminous wings

The mind is a sensing plate. According to its clarity, sensitivity and alignment, so will be the ability to register Light.

In order to sense Light, the mind has to be turned in the right direction. When aligned with the source of Light within, it can shed illumination upon all matters.

To keep the mind steady is difficult indeed. Mostly it does not remain poised for long enough to allow for that unruffled moment when Light can slip in.

But with practice and persistence, it will learn to attune to the sound of Light.

It is natural to move in the direction of Light. We are actually drawn to it and the glimpses encountered through life beckon us from the unfolding edge of our awareness.

In these high moments we dream of a sweeter world, one that is just and sane. We sense the awakening beauty, so ready to express itself.

Responding to this steadily increasing yearning from inside, we long to create a world in line with higher and more refined values, human ones.

The measure of Light we are able to apply determines the civilization we create. Stronger potencies of Light always demand new forms, and all progress requires that we relinquish what holds us back.

The fresh insights, broader views and higher values cannot be expressed through the outgrown, and in want of appropriate forms will remain only hopes and visions.

Our ingrained habit of perceiving everything in a broken and partial way, made us construct a world in our own distorted self-image.

Allured and engrossed with material desire, we ventured down the path of competition, exploitation, selfishness and greed, having not yet developed common sense.

This erroneous way of seeing prevents us from expanding beyond the present impasse of perilous cleavage; between man and man, nation and nation, and humanity and nature.

Without inclusive vision, we cannot see the picture Whole.

Do not think that caterpillar sleeps

It has finally arrived
at a point of

balance

focused
attentive

still

Inside the chrysalis

a concept having served its time
is becoming obsolete

Old certainties recede
false notions unravel

An image of self is coming apart

In the interlude

at a quiet point of
poise

the mind slips into a new perspective

Silent

there is no one here

only the Breath
and the beating of a Heart

so steady and so calm

Quiet

there is nothing here

only Life
listening

Almost impossible to discern
among the whispering voices

one that is
still

In the simplicity of nothing

a place of
instant

Unbroken
Uncorrupted
True

A Name Yet Unspoken

dwelling in the
clear, calm eyes

in the undisturbed mirror
at the end of words

Chrysalises hidden among dry leaves

Except for the keen eye
nobody takes any notice

A seed of Light
ignited in the dark

a place of sacred
a point of holy

tender like a bud

Light is the means by which Life is becoming aware of itself. Dispelling all that never was, it leaves us with nothing to conceal the Self with.

As the mind finally comes to its senses and resigns to the open space, a clear reflection is restored.

A swaying flower

the faint memory of
something else

There are Those who discovered the World of Light eons ago, while we were still asleep, deep in the soil of ignorance.

In the dark of night these Early Risers discerned a call, glimpsed a trail and pioneered into illumined fields, becoming that Light which They entered.

Spun through history runs a shimmering thread, weaving sense out of seeming chaos and forming a pattern of awakening beauty.

Glimmers of Truth, jewels of Pure, guiding us out of the maze, back from whence we came.

Great or small
dormant or expressed

the essence is the same

The difference is only
a matter of time

When Light breaks through

it first reveals the dust and dirt
so painful for the eyes

So many veils
obscuring the sight

so many layers of delusion

This little mind
constrained and
captured in its forms

This tiny flicker
so uncertain

Slowly forming petals of
sensing awareness

neither here nor there

Not belonging to one
nor the other

Cannot return
and cannot find

the way through

Only a trickle
of Light

Just bright enough
to glimpse

one step
at a time

You know there are sparrows
winding upwards
and seabirds gliding high

You have heard of
the hawk and the
eagle

and somewhere

Invincible Ones
gone beyond Light

What then
are the wings of
a tiny?

Nature needs no ideologies
creeds or dogmas

in order to
blossom

Under the steady impact of
the radiant sun

Life is expressed

in simple, unassuming
beauty

Little as the caterpillar can avoid
its destiny

no more can we

What is inherent
will become

and what kind of choice is
time, really?

Held in a seed
lies the unfoldment

held in a seed
is the coming

petal by petal
That Which Is

has no choice but
revelation

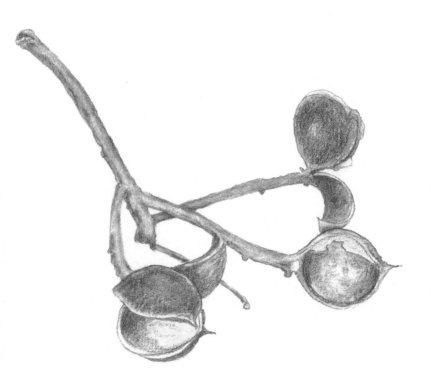

So many times
you passed Me by

not recognizing
The One

searching for you

So often you dismissed
My pleading eyes

begging for your
remembrance

For so long now
I have been calling

and time is weary

Hush

so many broken ones
with blurred eyes

Tears make no sound

Sometimes, a glimpse is not recorded immediately. It may take a long time before even the brightest ray of Light has penetrated all layers of delusion and finally registers in consciousness.

But suddenly, it will drop into awareness, so obvious and self-evident that we may wonder how it was possible to ignore for so long.

It is time.

Life is aspiring towards a new expression. It is bursting at the seams, cracking on the surface, having outgrown its old forms.

As the Light in the world increases, an ancient delusion is losing its hold and the mirage of the separate quickly dissolving.

Myriads of Sparks of Light, each a unique and unfolding aspect of an indivisible Whole, are emerging from the long incubation in the dark.

Eagerly pushing forward to build in accordance with a higher vision and create the forms and structures that will allow the true beauty of Humanity to shine through.

Have you noticed
how the most unsuspected moment

suddenly takes on
an unusual glow

alighted from within?

A World of Light
so thinly veiled

awaiting just beneath the dawn

Not the spectacular
flashing, loud events

nor the exotic
apparently so different

but the Quietly Unnoticed

so familiar
we did not even recognize

its utter holiness

The long forgotten
One

the Unbroken Promise

watching us patiently
from behind time

looking through
a multitude of eyes

trapped
among the sleeping

struggling
to emerge

Hidden where we could not see
too ordinary to notice

those eyes we've met
a million times

Petal by petal
unfurling

a new sound of
Joy

Petal by petal

drops of Real
the taste of Pure

Through rent webs

the first scent of
Grace

One day

there will be a fold in the day
where we will slip through

and for a hushed, timeless moment

find ourselves
in the Real and the True

One day

we will see
The One

Who has been waiting

for us to take
the first step

Those Eyes
like a mirror

holds before us
a reflection of

The Unbroken

One day
soon

we will gather our Light
and shine

Resting on a flower

those fragile wings of beauty
in the sun

For the first time
butterfly unfolds

having released its
sense of Self

from the claims of
the caterpillar

In a brief moment

aligning with the course of
unimpeded Light

Keeps nothing back
adds nothing to

Offering Light
on a tiny plate